Shrewsbury Abbey
A Medieval Monastery

Nigel Baker

Shropshire
Books

Front cover: The Abbey Church by Evacustes A Phipson, 1908.
Back cover: The Abbey Mansion and Pool by W W Gill, 1846
(Shrewsbury Museums).

© *Text Nigel Baker*
ISBN: 0-903802-75-9

Cover and book design: The Graphic Terrace
Managing Editor: Helen Sample
Published by Shropshire Books, the publishing division of
Shropshire County Council's Community & Economic Services Department

Printed in Great Britain by Livesey Limited

Contents

About the Author

Nigel Baker is a freelance archaeologist specialising (when permitted) in medieval towns. Work in Norwich, and as a Birmingham University student in Worcester, was followed in 1978 by a first encounter with medieval Shrewsbury, deep below the floors of the Castle Gates library buildings. After research at Nottingham University he spent three years co-directing a project excavating at Shrewsbury Abbey and in the town centre. Since completing a Leverhulme Research Fellowship in the School of Geography at Birmingham (looking at the Church in medieval towns), he has been engaged on the Shrewsbury Urban Archaeological Strategy Project, on behalf of the Borough and County Councils, and English Heritage. He and his family live in the countryside just outside Shrewsbury.

Acknowledgements

Much of what appears here draws upon the work of other archaeologists, archaeological scientists, historians, and other specialists who have studied Shrewsbury Abbey and the materials discovered in the excavations there, many of whom have contributed reports to the archaeological monograph. The author wishes, in particular, to acknowledge the work of: Victoria Buteux, Worcestershire Archaeology Service (pottery and other artefacts); Marion Campbell, Victoria & Albert Museum (the silver saucer); Bill Champion and Dorothy Cromarty (historical sources); Malcolm Cooper, English Heritage and Hugh Hannaford, Shropshire County Council, (the excavations); John Darlington, Stafford Borough Council (the ironwork and the excavations); Dr James Greig, University of Birmingham (botany); Gillian G Jones (animal bone); Steve Litherland, BUFAU (1993-94 investigations); Cameron Moffett (stone artefacts); Richard K Morriss (architecture); Quita Mould (leatherwork); David Pannett (masonry sources).

Grateful thanks are additionally due to: the Parish Church of the Holy Cross, Shrewsbury, and its vicar, the Rev. Ian Ross; Birmingham University Field Archaeology Unit, English Heritage, the Shrewsbury Museums Service; Arthur Fielder and the Shrewsbury Quest; the Archaeology Service, Shropshire County Council; Tony Carr, and the staff of the Shropshire Records and Research Centre.

The 1985-87 excavations were funded by British Rail, The Community Programme, Lichfield Diocese, English Heritage, Shrewsbury & Atcham Borough Council and Shropshire County Council.

The extract from 'To the Abbot of Shrewsbury' by Guto'r Glyn is taken from the translation by R Gerralt Jones, *The Poets of the Princes*, vol.I, Tern Press, Market Drayton, 1976.

Above all, this book could not have been written without the work of all the staff of the Shrewsbury Heritage Project, 1985-1988.

Picture Credits

Introduction

The Benedictine Abbey of St Peter and St Paul stood in the Foregate suburb of Shrewsbury for just over four hundred and fifty years, about the same span of time that separates us today from the abbey's closure in January 1540 by Henry the Eighth's commissioners. The greater part of the monks' church survives, saved for the use of the parish, but there is little else left standing as a visible reminder of the monastery that was such an important part of the county town for so many centuries. The abbey was founded in a suburb and, since its demise, the suburb has grown back over it, breaking through its precinct walls, and concealing the remains of its once substantial buildings beneath houses, gardens, a railway station and its inevitable successor, a car-park. Fragments of the monks' buildings do survive, separated from the church by the new main road of 1836.With the aid of written records, maps, and drawings made of the site before the most destructive changes of the nineteenth century, their meaning can, in part, be understood. Modern archaeological excavation began at the abbey in the 1980s and, with the analysis of the results, the long, slow process of finding out not just what the abbey was like at the end of its life, but how it changed during its life, is just beginning.

Chapter One

Shrewsbury Abbey in history

The beginning

Shrewsbury is a Saxon town. In the Roman period its river-loop hilltop site and the surrounding area would have been a mixture of scrub-covered slopes and farmland, part of the hinterland of the great regional capital at Wroxeter. Shrewsbury enters the documentary record incidentally in the year 901 when a royal grant of land to Wenlock Priory was witnessed there, an event that is most likely to have taken place at a royal hall. There had been two monasteries on the site for some time, perhaps as long as two centuries, and probably about this time another two were founded; there may also have been a small but growing permanent population making a living from trade or from crafts. Within a generation there was a mint as well, which by contemporary law could only have been set up somewhere that was protected by fortifications: the English place name Scrobbesbyrig may be translated as the fortified place in the district called the Scrub. A century later it was the shire town, and by the time of the Norman Conquest in 1066 there were five churches, a substantial population (perhaps around 1200-1500) and a suburb, the Foregate, was growing up across the river to the east.

In this suburb was a property belonging to one of the two wealthiest men in the county - Siward , sometimes referred to as the rich man of Shropshire, whose father had been a kinsman of Edward the Confessor. His hall stood on a site at the confluence of the Severn and the Meole or Rea Brook, and close by he had built a wooden chapel dedicated to St Peter. While this was said soon after the Norman Conquest to be the poorest of the town's churches, it seems actually to have been a moderately well-endowed private monastery; it also probably had a burial ground, as graves with skeletons laid on beds of charcoal, a distinctive late Saxon tradition, were found in the 1890s. After the Conquest, Siward pledged allegiance to King William and was allowed to keep a proportion of his estates, but surrendered his Shrewsbury property in return for the manor of Cheney Longville.

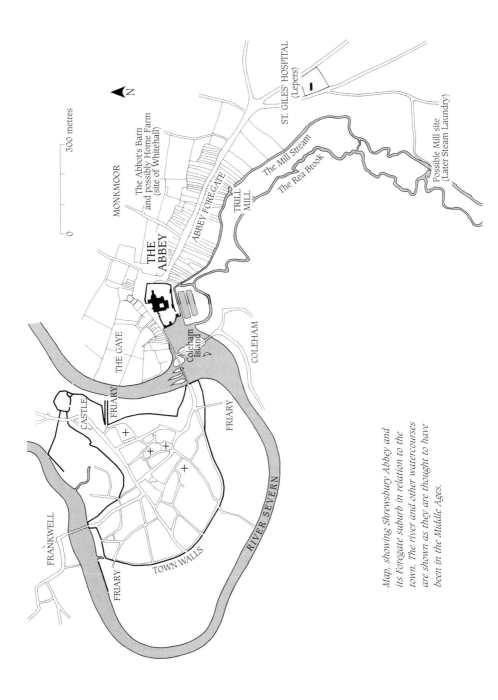

Map, showing Shrewsbury Abbey and its Foregate suburb in relation to the town. The river and other watercourses are shown as they are thought to have been in the Middle Ages.

In 1068 Roger of Montgomery was created Earl of Shrewsbury by King William, his close friend. Soon after, Roger gave St Peter's church to a priest in his service, Odelerius of Orleans. According to his son, the historian Orderic Vitalis, in 1082 Odelerius went on pilgrimage to Rome and returned having made a vow to rebuild the church in stone. In February 1083 Earl Roger, who was contemplating founding a monastery, was persuaded by Odelerius to take over and re-found St Peter's. Accordingly, Earl Roger made a public pledge to found an abbey, laying his gloves on the altar of St Peter's and granting to it the whole of the suburb outside the east gate. This suburb, now Abbey Foregate, effectively became the abbey's own borough, under the legal jurisdiction of the abbot and quite independent of the town. Building work on the new abbey began under the supervision of two monks from the Abbey of Seez, an earlier foundation by Roger, and was in progress when Domesday Book was compiled in 1086. The following year, regular monastic life began under Fulchred of Seez, the first abbot.

The site that was chosen for the new abbey was in some ways less than ideal. It was cramped, hemmed in by watercourses on two sides and by the main road on another, but its disadvantages may have been outweighed by other factors that had a particular appeal to Earl Roger. The site was of considerable tactical importance. It lay on a channel of the Severn, facilitating transport of supplies and building stone, and overlooked both the principal road into the town from the east, and the river crossing, though whether there was a bridge here at this date is uncertain. The Norman castle at Shrewsbury, built in the 1060s, had been sited so as to control the Saxon town by dominating the dry-land approach from the north. The townsmen had in fact risen in revolt in 1069, and laid siege to the castle in alliance with the men of Chester and Wales. On the western approach to the town is the suburb of Frankwell, originally Frank ville, a name of uncertain significance but one that undoubtedly represents a French presence of some sort. The abbey, dominating the eastern approach to the town, may, it seems, have been the final element in the Norman conquest of English Shrewsbury.

The abbey site also offered an unusual economic advantage, in that it lay at the end of the best milling stream for many miles around. Along with the Foregate suburb, three watermills (presumably once Siward's) were granted to the abbey at its foundation, and from the figures given in the Domesday survey these were amongst the most profitable mills anywhere in the country, with a virtual monopoly over the growing urban population. Otherwise, the new abbey was but moderately endowed with rural manors and churches to provide it with an annual income, and, according to William of Malmesbury, the first monks were short of food and clothing, though later gifts to the abbey improved matters. In 1094 Roger of Montgomery died, having taken monastic vows shortly before, and was buried between the two altars of his new abbey church.

Life in the abbey

Life in the abbey, for its resident community of monks, was governed by the Rule of St Benedict, and its daily routine of prayer and worship in the choir of the church, meals eaten in common in the refectory, and rest in the common dormitory. Shrewsbury was known for its scholarship, so we may also be justified in imagining the monks frequently engaged in reading, study, and copying in the north walk of the cloisters. But the documents that survive from the medieval abbey are overwhelmingly concerned with its external affairs, mainly its title to property and its rights and privileges as a manorial lord, and there is comparatively little contemporary evidence for what went on inside the monastic precinct. Some revenues from its property were however dedicated to the support of particular buildings and activities, and the documents that record these do at least confirm the existence of buildings that one would expect to have been there but are as yet unknown archaeologically, and they also give just a flavour of the day-to-day business of running the precinct. Tithes were for example sometimes allocated to the building of the church, and there are thirteenth-

An imaginative reconstruction of the interior of the monastic refectory showing the reader's pulpit. Drawing by Kathy Green.

century records of funds assigned to the almonry to accommodate the poor, the monks' kitchen, and the 'guardian of the works' (the monastic official in charge of the buildings); gifts were also made to the kitchen, the infirmary, and to specific altars or chantries within the abbey church, particularly the altar of St Mary in the Lady Chapel east of the high altar *(see p.29)*. In c.1245 the abbey bought property and divided its rents to support the fabric in general, the kitchen, the chantry and altar of St Mary, the infirmary, guest-house, almonry, and to the refectory for cups, cloths, and the repair of the staircase.

In comparison with other Benedictine monasteries, the abbey was neither large nor particularly wealthy, and its monastic community too was a small one. At the election of a new abbot in 1460 it numbered only twelve: the prior, sub-prior, and third prior, eight monks, including the cellarer, and the Prior of Morville, who was normally absent; when the abbey was dissolved in 1540 there were seventeen monks and the abbot. In addition to this small resident community of monks, there was an unknown number of paid monastic servants (the Benedictines not having lay brothers), and documents of various dates refer in passing to the janitor, the porter, the abbot's household servant, and the abbot's horse-keeper, and there were doubtless many others working in the precinct, and on the abbey's demesne lands (which it managed itself), on its home farm, and at its mills, though their numbers probably decreased later in the Middle Ages as such properties were leased out. We know something of the abbey servants' diet, from agreements between the abbey and its 'permanent guests' or corrodians - citizens who left property to the abbey in return for what would now be termed sheltered accommodation in the vicinity of the precinct in their old age. The guests' servants were to receive each day two servants' loaves (as distinct from the monks' loaves), two gallons of inferior ale, and one of the servants' dishes.

From time to time the permanent population at the abbey was swollen - and must occasionally have been vastly outnumbered - by visitors and temporary guests. Its location just outside the county town must have ensured a fairly continuous demand for accommodation from travellers, and from the poor seeking shelter in the almonry. Additionally, we can identify two particular groups of visitor: royalty, nobles, senior churchmen, and their officials and household staff having business in the town or with the abbot; and pilgrims, coming to the shrine of St Winefred. Royal and noble visitors and their officials often visited the abbey. The royal Exchequer was housed at the abbey for a time in the thirteenth century, and taxes collected in the county were stored there in 1344; Richard II lodged at the abbey and Parliament met there in January 1398; Henry V is said to have come on pilgrimage in 1416; Edward, Prince of Wales, stayed in 1479-80 and Henry VII in 1495. On each of these occasions visiting monarchs, noblemen and officials would have been accompanied by a substantial number of retainers and household staff together, of course, with their transport animals. All would require some kind of accommodation. We have no details of how this was organised at Shrewsbury, but historical evidence from other abbeys -

Bury St Edmunds and St Mary's Abbey, York, for example, suggests that the most important guests would have been entertained by the abbot himself and would have dined in his hall or private apartments, while lesser guests would have been the responsibility of the community and dined in the refectory or a separate guest hall. Distinctions were sometimes drawn on the basis of the number of horses in a guest's baggage train: at York, guests with less than twelve horses went to the guest house and were the responsibility of the cellarer (the monastic official responsible for provisioning), those with more were fed by the abbot.

The abbey also accommodated official guests of the town bailiffs, and some early sixteenth-century corporation accounts record the cost of their victuals, which the town paid for. For example, at Christmas 1520-1, the king's commissioners lodged at the abbey and received a present 'for the honour of the town' of a boar (8 shillings and 5 pence = 42.5p), two swans (8s / 40p), a quarter hogshead of claret (33s 4d / £1.67) and 'wine spent at tasting the said hogshead' (10d / 4.5p). Accounts for other visits in this period similarly feature swans, boars, and substantial quantities of wine. Such hospitality was not confined to V.I.P.s that the abbot, or the corporation, needed to impress. Some time in the fifteenth century the abbey was visited by Guto'r Glyn, an itinerant Welsh court poet who, doubtless singing for his supper, composed a poem in honour of the abbot:

...This month I've not lacked nutrition.
A certain feast has kept me late,
Double feast of this lord Abbot.
There's wine for a hundred to have,
Wine wouldn't let this one man leave.
His foster-child, could I refuse
This Abbot of Shrewsbury's largesse?
There flowed right to my marrow-bone
Fine raspberry wine or wine from Spain.
And his meals (heaven's very fee)
From this saint's board, glorified me.
The man does not hoard his riches
But shares his income three straight ways.
One for his hospitality,
On his hearth to offer freely;
The second to succour the weak;
The third to maintain the fabric
To hold court, make a fine building,
To teach the metres, promote learning.

And the impression of generous entertainment that these sources give is now supported by the archaeological evidence *(see Chapter Four)*.

A stone panel probably from the shrine of St Winefred (the central figure). After the Dissolution, it was re-used back to front on the gateway tower of the old English Bridge, then rescued and installed in a garden on Swan Hill, Shrewsbury. It is now back in the abbey church.

St Winefred

From the early twelfth century the abbey would also have played host to an unknown but possibly substantial number of pilgrims. The abbey had been founded in the 1080s on a site that was mainly secular; unlike many, it was not a re-foundation of an ancient religious house with a patron saint's relics already providing a focus for popular devotion, prayer, and offerings. So the new abbey set out to acquire its own saint. An account written by Robert, prior of the abbey (the most senior monk after the abbot) in the 1130s, describes how the monks 'very often lamented amongst themselves, that they were very deficient in relics of saints' and applied their minds to the problem of obtaining some. They had heard, he said, 'that the bodies of many saints were retained in Wales, which was near them', and while they were debating which saint they should acquire and honour, one of the monks was, as the Shrewsbury historians Owen and Blakeway put it, 'seized with a mental derangement'. The community prayed for his recovery and entreated neighbouring monasteries to do the same. While the monks at Chester Abbey were thus engaged, Ralph, their sub-prior, had a dream in which St Winefred, virgin and martyr, appeared and promised that the monk would be restored to health if mass was celebrated by the monks at her well (Holywell in Flintshire). This duly took place, the monk recovered, and the Shrewsbury community, now convinced that St Winefred was to be their patron saint, organised an expedition to recover her bones from their burial place at Gwytherin in Denbighshire. To cut a long story short, the party, led by prior Robert of Shrewsbury and the prior of Chester, was guided miraculously to her grave, unearthed her relics, and brought them back to Shrewsbury. They were deposited in the church of St Giles while the bishop's authority was sought for their installation at the abbey. The monks kept vigil, further miracles took place, and then,watched by a now vast crowd, the relics were taken in procession down the Foregate and placed on the altar of the abbey church.

St Winefred (Gwenfrewi, a celtic saint whose historical identity, even reality, is uncertain) was taken to Shrewsbury Abbey in c.1138 and there is no doubting her importance to the abbey in the following centuries. A new shrine for her relics was built in the abbey church by Abbot Nicholas Stevens in the later fourteenth century, and the carved masonry panel with three figures in niches, now in the abbey church, may be part of it. The relics of St Beuno, according to legend Winefred's uncle and spiritual mentor, were also taken illegally by the monks of Shrewsbury and added to the church. Henry V is said to have gone on pilgrimage, on foot, from Shrewsbury to Holywell in 1416 to give thanks for his victories over the French at Agincourt and Harfleur, and in 1463 Abbot Thomas Mynde established a chantry at her altar to pray for the soul of Henry and his heirs; in 1487 the same abbot set up a guild in her honour, recruiting its members from the wealthiest Shrewsbury citizens and their wives. Across the country, the cult of St Winefred appears to have been at its most popular in the late fourteenth and fifteenth centuries. At Basingwerk Abbey, Flintshire, which had administered Holywell since 1240 and was closely associated with the cult, late fifteenth-century literary sources describe the rebuilding of its housing for guests, who were said to be so numerous that they had to be accommodated at meals at two sittings, at which they were treated to a choice of wines from three countries. Our problem is that, while the cult was certainly promoted at Shrewsbury and would have attracted pilgrims, there is no internal evidence of them, or the numbers in which they came to the site, or the offerings that they would have made at her shrine. The architectural and archaeological evidence reveals ambitious rebuilding in the western parts of the precinct and the church at precisely the time that her cult was at its most popular, but we cannot at the moment distinguish between provision that the abbey may have made specifically for pilgrims, and all the other guests that we know for certain it entertained.

The abbey and the town

At first sight, the relationship between the abbey and its parent town that is apparent from the surviving records was a troubled one, even, on occasion, openly hostile. That this should be so is not particularly surprising, given that the abbey was an alien institution planted on the doorstep of an already ancient urban community and given lands, wealth, legal independence and particular privileges at the expense of its elder neighbour. Trouble was inevitable from the moment of the abbey's foundation. The first bone of contention between the two concerned their respective rights to mill corn.

Shrewsbury Abbey. Seen from the south-east, along the Rea Valley, the abbey still appears to look down from its raised site above the floodplain.

Aerial view of Shrewsbury Abbey, looking north. The 1985-87 abbey excavations are in progress in the foreground.

The abbey church and former precinct in 1847. Telford's new road had been built just over a decade before; the refectory pulpit and Abbey Mansion buildings may be seen to the left of the new road.

A

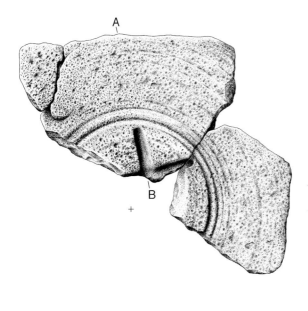

B
+

*Part of a millstone,
probably of Anglo-Saxon
date, from the 1985-87
Abbey excavations.
Drawing by Peter Dyke.*

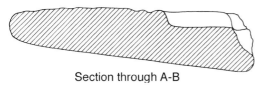

Section through A-B

Roger of Montgomery's early grants to the abbey included the three Foregate mills in the Rea Valley. As noted earlier, these mills were highly profitable to their owner because the growing urban population ensured a healthy demand for the grinding of corn into meal, and there was little scope for building successful rival watermills on the banks of the Severn (which is slower and has an enormous annual rise and fall), or on other streams. In 1121 the abbey was granted a charter by Henry I which converted this geographical monopoly into a legal one: all grain ground by the townspeople had now by law to be taken to the abbey's mills. This, the earliest legal milling monopoly on record, was doubly unusual in being applied across manorial boundaries - at the expense of the town and to the profit of the abbey - and was bitterly resented. The first hints that the townspeople were building illegal mills come in the 1220s, and matters came to a head in 1267 when the burgesses were, in Owen and Blakeway's words, 'prompted to spurn the slavish badge of their former subjection'. The abbot brought a legal action against the burgesses but, being out of favour at court for his recent support for Simon de Montfort against the king, had to be content with a compromise settlement in which the abbey's absolute monopoly was relaxed, the burgesses and the abbey were to share costs and profits alike for what were to become common mills, and the horse- and windmills built in the town allowed to remain. Still discontent, the burgesses neglected their obligation to the upkeep of the common mills, and built more unauthorised mills. Further legal actions followed in 1279-80, 1307, and as late as 1422, by which time the abbey was being forced to defend its milling rights in its own suburb.

Similar problems arose over the respective rights of the town and the abbey to hold annual fairs. Soon after its foundation the abbey had been granted the right to hold a three-day fair, which it did just outside the precinct in an open space laid out for the purpose; this was the area known later as Horsefair, now partly built over. A successful fair could attract traders and visitors from very far afield, but held next door to a permanent trading community it was a potential source of friction, just as today a Sunday market may be most unwelcome to a local Chamber of Commerce. The town got its own fair early in the thirteenth century, and in 1267, along with their victory over the abbot and his milling monopoly, secured from the king the right to hold a second fair. The duration of the abbey's fair, the rights of people coming to it and the tolls they were forced to pay passing through the town, all were the cause of further arguments, and were used as bargaining counters in other disputes. Not all such were settled in the courts. In 1401 the abbot commenced proceedings against thirteen townsmen who allegedly attacked the abbot's servants while they were collecting tolls at his fair. This was probably more significant than an average street brawl, given that these men included a 'gentleman', a draper, mercers and the town's M.P.

Boundary disputes between adjoining manorial jurisdictions are not uncommon in medieval urban history, and, sadly, nowhere was this more true than in Shrewsbury. The boundary between the town and the abbey was the River Severn, and herein lay much of the problem. The Severn was, and to an extent still is, fundamentally unstable, meandering and shifting its course almost year by year; islands appear as if from nowhere, banks are eroded, and channels silt up. Man-made structures also have an impact, and the effects of such works was understood by the medieval inhabitants who watched them jealously for their impact on the river as a boundary to their property, as a potential threat to their property, and as a shared economic resource. In 1255 the base of the mound of Shrewsbury Castle was eroded by the river, and testimony was given that it was the fault of the abbot's new mill on the opposite bank, where the football ground now stands. The Dominican (Black) Friars at the bottom of St Mary's Water Lane were in dispute with the abbey in the 1260s over the potential effect on the latter's riverbank of improvements made by the friars to theirs, and in the 1290s a settlement had to be reached concerning jurisdiction over four new islands that had arisen downstream from the Stone (English) Bridge. The most bitter quarrels concerned the limits of the abbey's and the town's jurisdiction over the bridge itself, and with an area of land known as Merivale, just west of the abbey on the site of the present Wakeman School. The Merivale dispute is first heard of in the 1480s, and was probably caused by the emergence of dry land on the bank of the old eastern Severn channel *(see p.36)* which was then silting up fast, making reclamation possible. The arguments were fought out in the courts, reaching the Court of Star Chamber in 1504, but spilled over into the streets and in 1510 Coleham Island, now Coleham Head, and Merivale were the scene of violent confrontations. According to the town bailiffs, the abbot's steward 'and other evil disposed persons' had assaulted and threatened the town sergeants, when out came the abbot and all his convent 'and other misruled persons to the number of sixty and above' to intimidate the sergeants and threaten them with imprisonment; furthermore, they said, Alan Mitton, the abbot's household servant, beat up one of the burgesses. In response, the abbot claimed that, having just publicly read out the court's latest decree in his favour, 28 named individuals had ridden into his franchise declaring that no-one was to obey it, or the abbot's manorial officers, nor should they attend the abbot's court; following which the town sergeant and the town catchpole remained there with their official maces and refused to go away. Later that year a further decision in the abbot's favour provoked the town bailiff and other officers into riding into the Foregate to attempt the arrest of John Passeffant, Crier of the Abbot's Court. When he resisted, they beat him, and his wife, and robbed him of his purse. A catalogue of further petty, vindictive little incidents followed, but the affair was largely settled in 1511-12.

Just a few years later we find in the Corporation account a record of three shillings spent on: 'Wine, apples, wafers and other new-fashioned dainties given and spent upon the Abbot of Shrewsbury and his servants for the honour of the town' at a play performed during Whitsun week 1516 in the old quarry behind the town walls (where the swimming baths now stand). For despite their quarrels, there is no doubt that the abbey was regarded as an asset to the town and its dignity, and the abbot played an important role in the town's ceremonies. The highlight of these was the annual feast of Corpus Christi, when a great procession, organised by the craft fellowships or companies made their way with great solemnity around the town and its suburbs. Its route is uncertain, though it would probably have started from one of the churches, possibly the abbey, and proceeded from there to the High Cross on Pride Hill before heading out to the suburbs, including Abbey Foregate. The tailors and skinners held their own procession a few days later, escorting their candle to the shrine of St Winefred at the abbey.

More tangible advantages to the town came from the abbey's presence. The abbey was far from being self-sufficient. Although agricultural produce would certainly have been supplied to it from its rural estates and home farm - particularly earlier on, before such enterprises were leased out - it is likely to have been a significant purchaser in the local markets. In 1504, in the course of one of their interminable disputes, the abbot rejected accusations by the bailiffs that the abbey was a cause of the town's current economic misfortunes, pointing instead to his annual expenditure of about 400 marks (£266) in the town on bread, drinks, and victuals; if this figure is reliable it would represent almost half of the abbey's annual income. Further statistics do not survive, but we can at least identify a range of goods and services that are likely to have been purchased locally and would have contributed to the town's economy. Pottery for instance. Cheap, but frequently replaced, this would have been a necessary purchase throughout the 450-year life of the abbey. We cannot prove that it was bought in the town markets, but the range of ceramics excavated at the abbey is almost the same as that found on domestic sites in the town centre. The main difference is in the absence of small domestic cooking pots at the abbey, probably because institutional catering called for big metal cauldrons and other vessels, and these too were made nearby in Coleham. The building industry - which would have encompassed labourers, masons, plumbers, daubers, carpenters, plasterers, painters, tilers, smiths, plus carters and boatmen to bring the materials to the precinct - would have been greatly stimulated by the episodes of rebuilding that can be identified at the abbey, and routine maintenance alone would have accounted for further work for these tradesmen, and the rural industries, forestry for instance, that supported them. As we have seen, the abbey was also a permanent employer of servants to run the precinct, though in what numbers we do not know.

There was also the abbey's role as the provider of hospitality and the buildings in which it could take place. A reliable guide to the town's estimation of this service (or at least to the usefulness of the abbey's buildings) may be found in the burgesses petition to the king at the Dissolution 'that the abbey may stand and remain to receive the prince's grace, or any other nobility of the realm that shall resort to this town'. So how, ultimately, was the demolition of the abbey regarded by the townspeople? Even its opponents in politics and religion would, thought Owen and Blakeway, 'scarcely behold without a sigh the subversion of an establishment, which, for so many successive generations, had furnished themselves and their forefathers with employment; had educated their youth, and relieved their poor'.

The Dissolution and after

The last years of Shrewsbury Abbey were not happy ones. Records of bishops' visitations to the abbey in the early 1500s show evidence of a decline from an orderly, well-maintained monastery where the monastic Rule was adhered to, to one split by internal dissent, tainted by financial irregularities and, at the end, disfigured by ill-maintained buildings. In 1518-1525 debts were found to be unpaid, accounts were not kept, and property was being leased out without authority. The dormitory was unlit and in bad repair and the second prior was accused of taking glass from the now derelict infirmary for his own lodgings. In 1536 it was alleged that there was by then no infirmary at all, the church roof over the high altar and the choir was leaking, and the abbot was even accused of pulling down monastery buildings and selling the materials for salvage. At this distance in time it is difficult to tell how far these allegations were justified, and how far they were motivated by a wider agenda.

On January 24th 1540, four of Henry VIII's commissioners arrived at the abbey to demand its surrender to the king. The abbot and the seventeen remaining monks met them in the chapter house and, having consented to the surrender, the abbey's seal was brought, some last documents were sealed, and it was then broken, and the monastery declared dissolved. The abbot, Thomas Boteler, and the monks were pensioned off.

The precinct was first leased by the crown and then in 1546 sold to speculators in monastic property. They then sold it on immediately to William Langley, a prosperous Shrewsbury tailor with diverse business interests. At this time many of the monastic buildings were demolished, or at least stripped of anything that was readily saleable. Some, however, were retained. The parochial nave of the abbey church was saved for the continuing use of the parish. The west range of the cloisters too was saved,

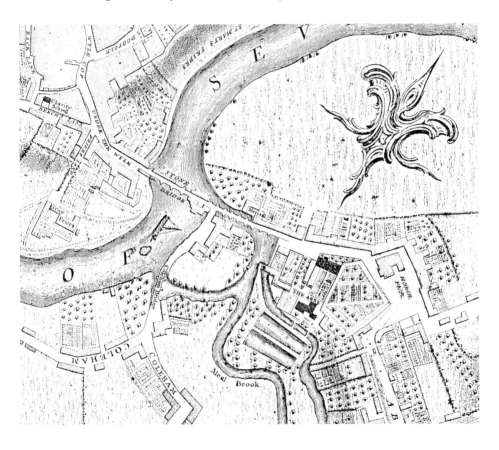

Extract from John Rocque's map of Shrewsbury, 1746. The Abbey Gardens occupy the open area east of the abbey church. To the south, the monastic fishponds and mill stream are seen in their original state.

and not long after part of it was rebuilt as a dwelling. Parts at least of the abbot's or other domestic buildings, including the former 'Guesten Hall' to the south of the refectory were retained by Langley for his own use, and later in the sixteenth century were modernised by the addition of a richly-decorated and jettied (overhanging) timber-framed building. This cluster of buildings, known later as the Abbey Mansion or simply as The Abbey, remained as the principal dwelling on the site until its demolition in 1866. To the west of the cloisters parts of the 'Old Infirmary' buildings were demolished or allowed to fall into ruin, though its north wing, on the old Abbey Foregate frontage, survived in domestic occupation *(see also pp.35-36)*.

The Langley family remained in possession of the site until the beginning of the eighteenth century. During their time, the old precinct became a place of fashionable recreation. The open space east of the church and in front of the Langley's mansion became the Abbey Gardens, laid out with gravel walks and planted with trees.

Plan of proposed building lots east of the abbey church in 1839. They are bounded to the north and east by the remaining precinct wall.

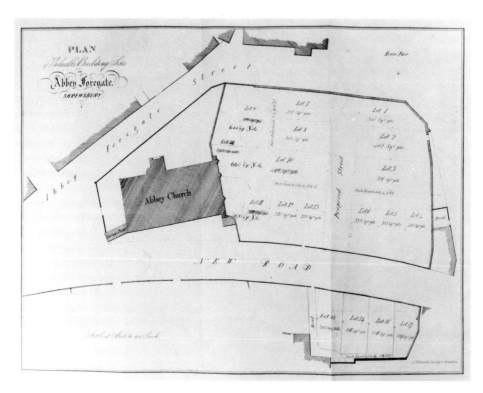

The Abbey Station.
Photographed probably
in the early 1920s.

Celia Fiennes visited Shrewsbury in 1698, and what impressed her most of all in the town were the Abbey Gardens. They were, she wrote, 'set full of all sorts of greens [evergreens] orange and lemon trees: I had a paper of their flowers were very fine, there was alsoe [aloes] firs myrtles and hollies of all sorts and a greenhouse full of all sorts of Curiosities of flowers and greens, there was the aloes plant; out of this went another garden much larger [the former cemetery] with several fine grass walks kept exactly cut and rolled for Company to walk in; every Wednesday most of the town the Ladies and Gentlemen walk there as in St James's Park and there are abundance of people of quality lives in Shrewsbury more than in any town except Nottingham'. The refectory pulpit probably owes its survival to the Langleys' enthusiasm for their gardens, when it was converted into a little glazed gazebo or summer house *(see p.30)*; something of the layout of the gardens themselves may be still be seen on John Rocque's 1746 plan of Shrewsbury *(see p.15)*.

In the early eighteenth century the site passed into the possession of the Powys family of Berwick. In the 1740s Henry Powys modernised the mansion and cleared the surrounding area of some ruined buildings, including fragments of the church choir and transepts and the probable almonry buildings west of the cloisters. But this 'tidying up' process was as nothing compared to the destructive impact of Thomas Telford's road through the precinct in 1836. Telford had been engaged in 1810 to improve the London to Holyhead road, which, following the Act of Union between Britain and Ireland at the turn of the century, had seen a steady increase in traffic. After the Welsh section of the road was improved, attention turned towards Shrewsbury, and in particular, the dangerous blind corner where the road followed the old precinct wall around the north side of the abbey. The new road formed a short cut, taking traffic straight to the approach to the English Bridge diagonally across the former cloisters; the northern half of the 'Old Infirmary', most of the west range of the cloisters and part of the precinct wall were all demolished.

The creation of a main road across the precinct presented new commercial opportunities for developing the area, and in 1839 it was decided to auction the land either side in small lots for building. However, a local consortium opposed to building on the open space around the abbey raised the money to purchase the land, and in 1840 formed a public cemetery company. Despite the overcrowded state of the town's churchyards, this was ultimately unsuccessful, though the open space remains to this day, having been sold to the parish for use by the abbey church. Across the new road, work began in 1866 on the construction of a terminus for Richard Samuel France's short-lived Potteries, Shrewsbury, and North Wales Railway Company. The new station occupied a narrow strip of land down the east side of the former precinct, but ground was cleared over a much larger area, the Abbey Mansion being demolished at this time, and the refectory pulpit saved only by the vigilance of the parish. At the same time the Abbey Pool, the former monastic fishponds, was filled in. It was this episode that effectively transformed the site of the precinct into the state in which it survives today.

The Abbey Mansion and pool, from the south. Watercolour by W W Gill, 1846.

An imaginative reconstruction
of Shrewsbury Abbey.

This picture shows the medieval
abbey from the south-west,
as it may have looked in the
fifteenth century. It is spring time:
the leaves are on the trees but
the level of the river in the eastern
channel of the Severn (foreground)
is still high. Boats are delivering
goods and visitors to the landing
stage of the buildings we know as
the 'Old Infirmary' in the abbey's
court or curia. Across the court
are the monastic cloisters.
Beyond, secluded from the outside
world, are the monks' dormitory,
the abbot's apartments and the
monks' cemetery; the monastic
infirmary is in the corner of the
precinct.

This reconstruction is based on
the surviving abbey buildings,
together with illustrations of
former buildings now demolished,
archaeological discoveries, maps,
documents and the evidence of
better-preserved monastic sites.
There are likely to have been many
more buildings than shown here.
Buildings left uncoloured are
purely hypothetical - though we
know they must have existed
somewhere in the precinct.
Painting by Chris Brown.

Above: The abbey church. Three main periods of work are visible: the west end of c.1360-80; the Norman nave of c.1100; and Pearson's east end of the 1880s.

Left: The abbey church, looking east.

Chapter Two
Shrewsbury Abbey today
Around the site

So much has changed on and around the site of the abbey since its dissolution in 1540 that it is difficult enough to trace the outline of the old precinct, let alone recapture the impression of a cluster of great stone buildings towering over the fortified precinct wall and dominating the low-lying watery suburb and its timber buildings. The single most destructive episode since 1540 was the construction in 1836 of Thomas Telford's new road straight through the remains of the cloisters, cutting off the church and the green open space of its cemetery from the remains of most of the former precinct. Now, fragments of only two of the medieval abbey buildings survive above ground south of the new road. One is the refectory pulpit, once part of the monastic dining hall that stood across the cloisters from the church. The other is the gabled red sandstone building known to archaeologists as the 'Old Infirmary' - though it was no such thing; this and the eighteenth-century Queen Anne House, stand within the Shrewsbury Quest centre, surrounded by modern timber-framed buildings that attempt to re-create the enclosed feeling of a cloister for today's visitors. Much of the area south of the main road is given over to car parking, a flat featureless sea of tarmac that completely disguises the dense archaeological remains and the original natural topography that lie beneath it. Close to the modern main road, a little behind the refectory pulpit, lies the southern edge of the monastic precinct and the sites of many sandstone buildings clustered within the precinct wall. Beyond, in line with the back wall of the Shrewsbury Quest, the ground once sloped gently downhill to meadows, a millstream and fish ponds that lay next to the Rea Brook. The brook is still there, running in a deep channel along the south side of the car park, but the fishponds were finally filled-in in the 1860s when thousands of tons of earth and rubble were dumped over the area, raising the ground level by many feet, to keep (it was hoped), a new railway works well above flood level.

There is a clearer boundary to the west side of the abbey site, formed by the Victorian railway viaduct and the modern road that runs between it and the remains of the 'Old Infirmary'. Where the road and the railway run today, there was once a channel of the river Severn. In the later Middle Ages it must still have been navigable, but it had been slowly silting up for centuries; reduced first to a stream, and by c.1800 to a stagnant dead end; the last trickle of open water was culverted in the 1930s *(see p.36)*.

THE ABBEY CHURCH

The abbey church is today the Parish Church of the Holy Cross. What survives is but a part of the medieval abbey church, saved in 1540 for the use of the parish, with some Victorian rebuilding of the roof and the east end. In the later years of the monastery's life the church would have been about 290 feet (88 metres) long; it is now about 208 feet (63 metres) long, including the rebuilt east end. As the monastic church it had transepts projecting north and south from the main body of the building (the nave), and where they met at the crossing, there was a central tower. The transepts, the crossing and its tower, and the choir, chancel and Lady Chapel at the east end were either demolished at the Dissolution or stripped of their roofs and fittings, and left to decay or be quarried for building materials.

The Exterior

Like many ancient buildings, the remains of the abbey church represent several periods of construction. The earliest dates back to the years either side of 1100 AD and the first great campaign of building when the abbey was founded. The base of the outside walls, and the semi-circular triforium arches visible in the upper part of the walls above the aisle roofs belong to this first phase: the masonry used was the local 'Keele Beds' sandstone, varying in colour from purple to browns and greys and cut into distinctive small squarish blocks. The second major phase of work came in about 1360-1380, the beginning of a period of extensive rebuilding around the monastery. The west end of the church dates to these years: the surviving west tower was built then, with a pair of tall pointed windows in its side walls and the great window in the west front, one of the most familiar images of Shrewsbury Abbey. No contemporary building accounts survive, but similarities in the detailing of the tower and its windows with work in Lichfield Cathedral and elsewhere have led to the suggestion that it was the work of a master mason by the name of William Driffield, whose career can be followed in major churches around the country in the later fourteenth century. A different sandstone was used in this period, a softer, darker brown stone (Bridgnorth sandstone) from the abbey's estates at Eyton-upon-Severn, a few miles down river, where the overgrown riverside quarry may still be found, with a boat dock cut into the natural sandstone for loading straight onto barges.

A great deal of the church was restored or rebuilt by the Victorians. The roof, the uppermost tier of windows (the clerestory), and the glazing of the arches below (the triforium) are all of nineteenth-century date. The east end and transepts were built in 1886-8 by J. L. Pearson R.A., better known as the architect of Truro Cathedral. For lack of sufficient funds, Pearson's original scheme for the complete reconstruction of the monastic east end could not be completed, and the transepts were left much shorter than originally intended. Their side walls were therefore finished to give the appearance of truncated ruins, both to blend in with the real ruined portions of the original transept walls surviving at ground level, and so that, when funds allowed, new masonry could easily be keyed in and the work continued.

The real remains of the medieval south transept facing the main road are easily distinguished, at least close to. The weathered stones of the early Norman builders contrast clearly with the sharp projecting orange-brown blocks of Pearson's mock ruin. Two arched doorways at ground level are, in fact, knocked-through cupboards, known as armarii, for storing books and writing materials for use nearby by monks working in the north walk of the cloisters. About 15 feet (4.65m) above ground level, at the junction of the church and the transept wall, is the last surviving projecting sandstone corbel, one of a series that would have supported the top of the cloister roof. On the other side of the church, the recently-restored remains of the medieval north transept may similarly be distinguished from the curtailed replacement work of the 1880s. Here, the ruined transept wall of c.1100 incorporates a window with simple tracery of the early 1300s, inserted into a Norman window opening. This also appears in one of the earliest drawings of the abbey *(see p.26)* made by Francis Sandford in 1658, a drawing which shows other features that have since disappeared. The remains of the transept then survived to a much greater height, and two of the original Norman windows are shown above the surviving one. At the junction of the transept with the church nave is all that then remained of the central tower, and in the upper part of the nave wall the original clerestory windows still survived just below the parapet (the present ones are late Victorian replacements). The north porch has changed relatively little. This too is a multi-period structure. The ground floor and vault were built in front of the Norman north door in the thirteenth century; the upper storeys date from the early fifteenth, using the brown Bridgnorth-type stone for the walls and the better grey-buff Grinshill stone for the detailing. One statue, said to be of St Margaret, remains in one of the niches flanking the first-floor window.

The Interior

The visitor to the interior of the church enters at the west end, either through the door in the west front, or through the Norman south door. At the west end, the tower and the first two pointed arches of the ground-level nave arcades belong to the building campaign of c.1360-80. High up in the tower, investigations by the church's engineers

*Our earliest view of the abbey church, by Francis Sandford,
1658. On the left, the stump of the old central tower may
be seen together with the upper windows of the ruined north
transept. The Norman clerestory windows survived at that date,
above the blocked arches of the removed triforium gallery.*

in 1997 discovered what is probably the medieval belfry floor, surviving sandwiched
between later floor surfaces on top and Victorian panelling beneath. The floor was
found to be constructed with massive oak timbers laid side-by-side, almost eaten
away by death-watch beetle, with the remains of the medieval bell-frame pegged to it:
this is the last surviving woodwork of the medieval abbey.

Beyond the west tower, the nave of the church is substantially early Norman,
the original arcades of large plain cylindrical piers supporting simple semi-circular arches.
Originally these arcades would have continued along the whole length of the nave, six
pairs of arches with a longer rectangular pier half way along, but the three westernmost
arches on each side were replaced in the fourteenth century rebuilding; their truncated
remains are still visible, embedded in the later masonry. The rectangular piers at the
junction of the Norman and the fourteenth-century work probably mark the position
of the medieval rood screen, in front of which the parish altar would have stood.
The screen would have divided the west end of the nave, used by the people of the

parish for their worship, from the remainder, which would have been the sole preserve of the monks. Above the nave arcades are the triforium arches, also part of the first phase of Norman construction. These arches now light the interior from the outside but would originally have been unglazed, giving access to long, covered triforium galleries over the side aisles. Little is known about these galleries; examples survive elsewhere, but at Shrewsbury they had gone by the 1650s at the latest and had presumably been cut short when the west end was rebuilt in the fourteenth century. Above the triforium arches are the clerestory windows, Victorian replacements of the Norman originals.

Either side of the nave are the aisles, also part of the original building, though their windows and roofs have been extensively rebuilt. Surviving shafts, capitals, springings, and scars on the masonry of the side walls show that the aisles must once have had stone vaults, though it is thought that these may have been taken out at an early date. The windows of the north aisle were replaced in the fourteenth century, possibly in c.1360-80 when the west end was rebuilt, and were enlarged and modified in the 1720s, probably when the present gabled roof above them was built. The wall beneath them was badly damaged during the Civil War, and several 'breaches' in it had to be repaired in 1649-52, having previously been blocked up with thorn bushes. At the east end of this aisle is a fine early Norman arch, stilted to form a raised semi-circle, on heavy cushion capitals; there is also a serpent carved on the north side of the base. This arch led, before the Dissolution, into the north transept. It was on this line that the demolition of the church stopped in 1540. As a result, the further (east) side of the arch is weathered and eroded, having been part of an outside wall from the Dissolution until the 1880s, when the new east end was built.

The south aisle is also largely the original Norman work from the first years of the abbey, though the arch at its east end (which would have led into the south transept) was replaced and enlarged in the late fourteenth century. It has been suggested that this arch was made wider because it was on one of the most frequently used processional routes in the church: close by it, behind the tomb said to be of Roger of Montgomery, is a low, broad, arched recess in the south wall. Although later rebuilt and altered, this occupies the site of the doorway through which the monks would have entered the church, in procession, from the east walk of the cloisters. The tomb and effigy traditionally said to be those of Earl Roger of Montgomery, the abbey's founder, are something of a mystery. The figure, though damaged, is clearly that of a knight, with chain mail armour, a surcoat, a long shield and a sword. The style of the effigy and the tomb on which it rests is thirteenth century, though Roger died in 1094, at the end of the eleventh. As the abbey's founder, he would undoubtedly have been buried in the church in a place of the greatest distinction, probably in that part which was demolished at the Dissolution: a contemporary account tells us that he was buried 'between the two altars'. The tomb attributed to Roger was evidently buried when the east end was demolished. In 1622 the College of Heralds visited the church, discovered the tomb in the ruins, and identifying it as Roger's, had it re-instated in the church close to where it now stands.

The search for the monks' east end

Historians of Shrewsbury Abbey have long wondered what the eastern parts of the monastic church looked like, and how they were arranged. The last ruins were probably levelled in the 1740s, before the earliest known drawings or maps were made, and a single document provided the only clues. This is a plumber's (lead worker's) account, dating from the time of the Dissolution, that gives a rough, back-of-an-envelope, estimate of the size of the lead roofs of the abbey buildings that were about to be stripped and melted down for their scrap value. It does not include roofs made of other materials, like stone slates, which would have been the majority, and it does not explain how the roofs lay in relation to each other. Nevertheless, it is a valuable source, and used in conjunction with recent archaeological investigations, it provides a general idea of the extent of that part of the church that lies buried beneath the Victorian east end and the grass outside. It gives, for example, the dimensions of the roof over the former central tower (30 feet square); lengths of the north and south 'aisles' of the church - by which it actually seems to have meant the old transepts; and east of the central tower, the length and breadth of the monks' choir and chancel, extending in all some 99 feet (30.15m) beyond the surviving medieval nave.

The first glimpse of the monastic east end for perhaps two centuries came in 1992. Drains taking rainwater away from the church roofs and downpipes required renewing, so the trenches for the new drains were dug by archaeologists. Just beyond the north-east corner of the Victorian chancel a trench picked up massive drystone foundations, crossing the trench diagonally. The foundations seemed most probably to be those of an apse - a semi-circular projection to a church (or other building), and a common feature of Norman ecclesiastical architecture. Moreover, the dimensions of the apse, when projected from the section exposed in the trench, coincided with those given in the plumber's account for the former chancel.

In many great churches Norman apsidal ends were demolished and replaced by great rectangular chancels in the course of ambitious building campaigns in the thirteenth century (at Worcester Cathedral, for example). Was this the case at Shrewsbury Abbey? Two seasons of geophysical survey provided a tentative answer, without further excavation. In 1995, the lawns east of the abbey church were surveyed using a resistivity meter, recording variations in the electrical resistance of the soil caused by buried anomalies: high resistances in waterless hard areas (buried wall-footings, floors); low resistances in softer, water-retentive deposits (infilled ditches, for example). The computerised plot of the readings revealed a buried anomaly extending eastwards from the apse, but too narrow to represent a substantial building like a thirteenth-century chancel. The following year, a survey by Keele University covered exactly the same ground with ground-penetrating radar, bouncing signals off buried features - walls, floors, earth strata - to produce a series of vertical slices through the survey area. The results broadly confirmed those of the resistivity survey. The radar found, first of all, a buried anomaly conforming to the predicted line of the apse, running under the row of monuments outside the Victorian chancel. Secondly, it confirmed the presence of further hard, reflective, targets extending to the east over a relatively narrow area. Comparison of the geophysics plots with the plans of other churches suggests strongly that the original Norman apse survived until the abbey's dissolution in 1540.

It was not replaced, but it was extended, almost certainly by a Lady Chapel. The cult of the Virgin became increasingly popular towards the end of the twelfth century and, particularly in the thirteenth, chapels were built and dedicated in her honour, usually at the east end of a church and often projecting eastwards from it (as, for example, at Tewkesbury and Gloucester). These results offer some confirmation of an impression given by the documentary sources, and what is known of the other abbey buildings: although Shrewsbury Abbey was one of the county's major landowners, and was of immense importance locally, it was never in the first league of Benedictine abbeys and lacked the surplus funds that others may have enjoyed. Its monastic community of twelve to eighteen monks was small in comparison with, say, Much Wenlock which had forty, so unlike the latter it did not need a huge monastic choir. After five hundred years many of its original Norman buildings were still in use - extended, and adapted, but never replaced.

The refectory pulpit. A photograph taken before 1866, when the jettied sixteenth-century building behind was demolished.

The refectory pulpit

Standing in its own garden immediately across the main road from the abbey church is the refectory pulpit. This is an octagonal structure built of Grinshill stone, the finest locally available for carved and decorative work, standing on and projecting from a short length of red sandstone wall. It was formerly an integral part of the south wall of the monastic refectory, and from it, sacred texts would have been read to the monks during meal times *(see p.4)*. The openings on the north side (facing the church) would have opened in the refectory interior; the openings on the south were glazed, admitting light from the outside. The steps up to the pulpit would have been within an arcaded passage in the thickness of the wall, with a glazed window facing out. A very similar pulpit may be seen in the surviving refectory at St Werburgh's Abbey, Chester a great open hall of striking proportions that gives some impression of what has been lost at Shrewsbury.

The pulpit dates from the early fourteenth century, possibly the 1320s or 1330s. Each of the panels below the interior openings were carved with a pair of figures: St Mary and Gabriel (the Annunciation), St Peter and St Paul, to whom the abbey was dedicated, and St Winefred and St Bueno. The original panels, sadly, were vandalised and removed in the 1990s, and the present panels are cast replicas; the restored originals may be seen at Rowleys House Museum. The pulpit ceiling has an intricately elaborate floral boss at the apex of the vaulting ribs, with a carved crucifixion scene.

Given that the pulpit was once part of a much larger building, a number of questions naturally arise: why does it have its own roof and when was this added? When was the rest of the refectory demolished and why was the pulpit alone saved? Not all can be answered, as no deep excavation has taken place here since before 1816, although part of the story is clear. The pulpit was preserved to be used as a fashionable garden ornament - a summer-house or gazebo. It stands in what was formerly the garden of the Abbey Mansion, the group of stone and timber-framed buildings that was developed as the residence of William Langley, the abbey's first lay owner after the Dissolution. Close inspection shows that, as well as its roof, the pulpit's north-facing (formerly internal) openings had once been glazed, as the jambs to the openings contain sockets for inserted iron bars to which leaded lights would once have been wired. The pulpit was also provided with a lockable door. In short, the pulpit was made into a weatherproof free-standing building, a romantic ruin, but somewhere to sit, enjoy the view and pass the time. What is less certain is whether it is on its original site, and how long the rest of the refectory stood before it was demolished. Summer-houses and gazebos were becoming fashionable towards the end of the sixteenth century, so it is possible that the refectory, or its ruins, survived that long; only excavation would provide a definitive answer.

The north side of the abbey church in 1788. A watercolour by the Rev. Williams.

The Queen Anne House site excavation.
The square stone building, built across the earlier
precinct wall, is thought to have been a kitchen
for preparing food for the abbey's guests.

Where the excavated kitchen walls were built over floodplain mud, they were supported on alder piles. These, and other organic materials, survived in the waterlogged ground.

Right: Excavated shoes. Working footwear, worn out, discarded by cobblers working in the precinct.

Below: Excavated shoes. The range of sole sizes demonstrates that women as well as men had their footwear repaired here.

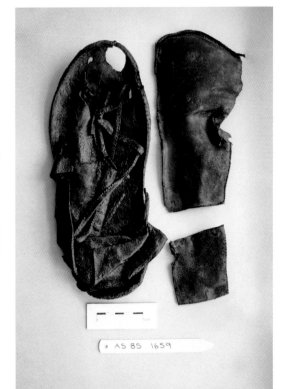

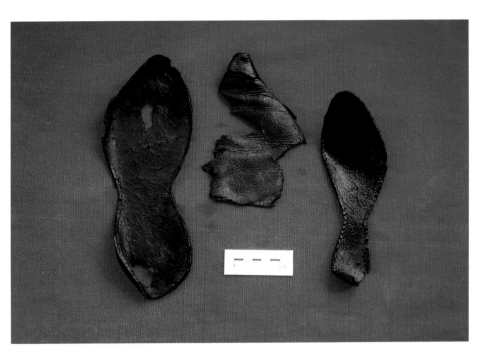

Engraving by Samuel and Nathaniel Buck
of the abbey, 1731. The remains of the main gate
can be seen to the right of the church on the old
(pre-Thomas Telford) Abbey Foregate frontage.

The 'Old Infirmary'

Within the Shrewsbury Quest visitor centre, on the western edge of the abbey site,
stands the remains of an enigmatic red sandstone building, one that appears to be
without parallel in English monastic architecture. This was known to nineteenth-
century scholars as 'The Old Infirmary' though it was almost certainly no such thing.
As it now stands, it consists of a two-storey building with a single room open to
the roof (the Quest's 'scriptorium') on the upper floor, lit by a large window in its
western gable end, and accessible via a medieval door at its opposite end, reached
by an external staircase. The ground floor is much lower, now partitioned off into
smaller rooms, the most notable feature being a great semi-circular blocked arch in
its south wall. Attached to this building on its north side are the remains of another,
best seen from the main road outside. This northern addition is represented by
a buttressed wall, obviously truncated, built of larger blocks of brown sandstone,
adjoining the gable end of the main block. Between its buttresses are small
rectangular windows at what are now ground and first-floor levels; a close look
at the base of the wall between the buttresses also reveals the top of a blocked,
pointed arch just above pavement level, with half of a second arch just where the
wall is truncated. Behind this (within the Shrewsbury Quest) is a much later brick
building housing a modern staircase and lift.

Many of the eighteenth- and early nineteenth-century drawings and engravings of
the abbey show this building much nearer to its medieval state. Before the new road
was built in 1836 the Old Infirmary was roughly twice its present size, the surviving
gabled building (the south range) being one of a pair, joined by a long buttressed
range of four bays, with a pointed arched doorway at the base of each.

The existing remains of the 'Old Infirmary'.

From these early illustrations an accurate reconstruction can be made of the west elevation *(see p.38)*, though there are very few views to show how these building ranges appeared from other directions. Neither is there much information from archaeological excavation inside. However, excavations nearby shed invaluable light on the original surroundings of the Old Infirmary and thus indirectly gave a clue to one of its original functions. In 1987 digging began just outside the Old Infirmary on the site of the Abbey Mill *(see p.63)*. The excavation revealed, under the mill, deep, wet, grey mud, deposited in what had once been a channel of the river Severn. When the Old Infirmary was built, it stood directly on this river channel. Moreover, the low level of the large arch in the south wall suggests that it may have given access to a slipway or dock along the south side of the building. The row of arched doorways in the western elevation must also have given access from the interior to the river, probably with some kind of timber landing-stage outside. From the depth of the channel found by the excavation it is probable also that it would have been navigable in the Middle Ages, though it was slowly silting up during the lifetime of the abbey. It seems fairly certain that the lower storey of the Old Infirmary ranges functioned as a covered waterfront, accommodating the movement of goods, and people, coming and going to the abbey via the river.

How the upper storeys were arranged, and how they were used, is less clear. The upper room of the surviving range (the Quest's 'scriptorium') seems always to have been a single large room, a first-floor hall. From the appearance of the large window in the gable end of the north range, demolished by Telford in 1836, there appears to have been another there. How the upper storey of the buttressed range linking the two was arranged, we have no idea: it may have been one long room, it may have been partitioned into a row of individual chambers. The only clue as to what these upper rooms may have been used for is the general setting of the Old Infirmary. Evidence is accumulating that this part of the monastic precinct was largely devoted to the accommodation of visitors to the abbey: visitors from every walk of life, royalty and nobles, ecclesiastics, government servants, and their household staff, and pilgrims, and paupers *(see pp.5-6)*. All would have been fed and housed in facilities that were to a large extent segregated, requiring a number of ranges of buildings. The most likely use of the upper storeys of the Old Infirmary was as part of such accommodation.

Archaeological analysis of the standing masonry of the Old Infirmary has shown that the gabled south range was built first, probably around 1280-1310, to judge from drawings of the tracery that once stood in the west gable window *(see p.63)*.

*The 'Old Infirmary', sketched by John Buckler
in 1813. The waterfront arches are clearly visible.
The half of the building nearer the artist was
demolished by Thomas Telford in 1836.*

5 metres

0

A Observed base of South Range footings c.47.50m
B Possible dock floor slabs, 43.76m
C Floor surfaces south of South Range, 50.22m
D Possible parapet level, fourteenth-century precinct wall

E Modern internal floor, South Range 51.45m
F Excavation: Jones 1989
G Conjectural mean water-level
H Modern ground level

The 'Old Infirmary': a reconstruction of the west elevation showing the surviving fabric in relation to what is buried, and what has been demolished.

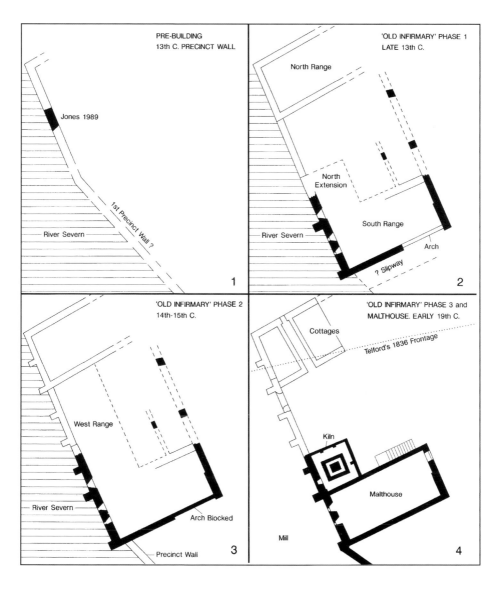

The historical development of the
'Old Infirmary'. Much remains obscure;
were this building to be fully excavated,
the story would undoubtedly be more
complex than presented here.

On its north side was an extension, possibly a private chamber attached to the hall, which was stone-built at ground-floor level but timber-framed above. This chamber was replaced by the long, buttressed, west range, but its former existence is given away in the western elevation by the northward continuation at ground level of the purple Keele Beds south range masonry to include one side of a former window opening that was truncated when the west range was built: this can be seen from inside the Quest. The buttressed range with its row of waterfront doorways made use of the kind of softer, larger blocks of Bridgnorth sandstone employed to rebuild the west end of the church in c.1360-1380; it may date from the same period or, more likely, to a few years after c.1400.

Nothing quite like the Old Infirmary is known from other English monasteries, though some others founded on riverside sites had free-standing, covered watergates: gatehouses built over a slipway (as at Worcester Cathedral Priory) or over an artificial water channel (as at Pulls Ferry, Norwich Cathedral precinct). However, more examples of the kind of waterfront architecture represented by the Old Infirmary can be seen in sixteenth and seventeenth-century panoramas of the City of London, stretching along

Watercolour by J Holmes-Smith showing the 'Old Infirmary' in its malthouse phase, c.1810. Note the louvre on the roof of the malting kiln to the right.

*The former abbey precinct court or curia,
now the Shrewsbury Quest. On the left is the
eighteenth-century Queen Anne House; to its right
the medieval sandstone 'Old Infirmary' building.*

the commercialised and densely built-up north bank of the Thames; the resemblance
of the blocked arch in the Old Infirmary's south wall to the Traitors' Gate in the Tower
of London is remarked upon by many visitors.

A little is known of the later history of the Old Infirmary. The north range, on the
old Abbey Foregate frontage, remained in residential use until its demolition in 1836.
The buttressed west range with its row of waterfront arches was probably the first
to go - only its west wall survived by the early eighteenth century when the first
drawings were made. The surviving south range was converted into a malthouse in
about 1800: extra floors were introduced within it for spreading the sprouting barley,
and the brick building still attached to its north side was built as the malting kiln where
the grain was roasted. Later, this part of the site became a builder's yard. Business was
interrupted in 1906 when the Abbey Mill was destroyed by fire and the Old Infirmary
was gutted. Latterly the buildings were used by a timber merchant. In 1993-94 the
Old Infirmary buildings were restored, following the archaeological analysis of the
phases of building that can be deduced from the masonry, and following a number
of small-scale excavations. New timber-framed buildings for the Shrewsbury Quest
were built, their design incorporating features found in the traditional timber-frame
architecture of the Shrewsbury area.

The Queen Anne House

Also standing within the Shrewsbury Quest site is the early eighteenth-century brick house generally (if inaccurately) known as the Queen Anne House. For a relatively recent addition to the abbey site, its origins are surprisingly obscure. It first appears on Rocque's map of Shrewsbury published in 1746, by when it had been standing for perhaps ten or twenty years. In the early eighteenth century ownership of the old precinct passed from the Langleys to Edward Baldwin, a friend of the last Mr Langley, and thence to the Powys family, the most likely builders of the Queen Anne House. The principal residence on the site was still the Abbey Mansion, so why and for whom a second residence was built is unknown. The Queen Anne House began as a five-bay building, with central back and front doors and two windows either side at ground and first-floor levels in the south elevation, lighting a single room on each floor flanking the entrance passage and stairs. After a very short period of time the building was extended to the west by a further two bays, the junction between the two phases of work still clearly apparent as a vertical joint in the brickwork. The building was again extended westwards later on when a lower service wing was added. By the 1820s, the house was owned and occupied by James Hiles, who ran the Abbey Mill a few yards away, and let out the Old Infirmary as a malthouse.

Medieval pottery from the 1985–87 excavations: table jugs, ceramic bottles and dripping pans.

Shrewsbury Abbey

National Grid intersections at 50m intervals

Key

- Medieval
- Post-Medieval
- Cartographic Evidence
- 19th Century
- Former water channels & ponds

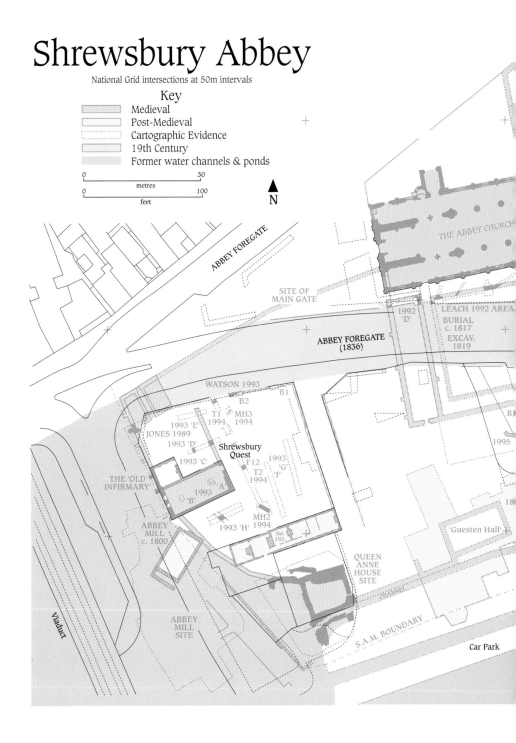

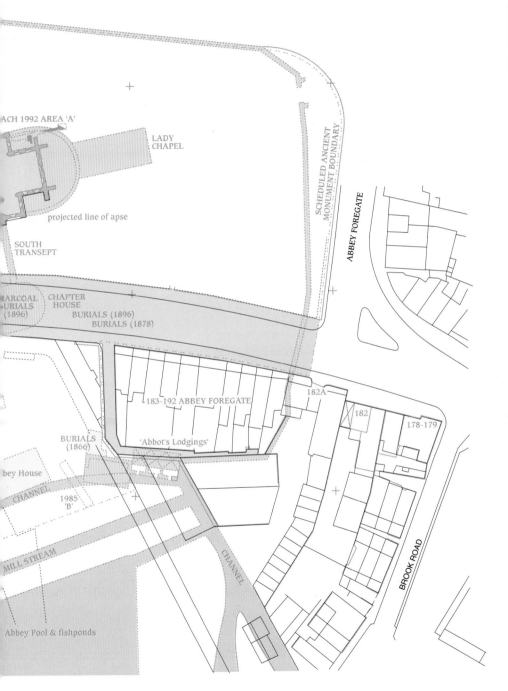

ACH 1992 AREA 'A'

LADY
CHAPEL

projected line of apse

SOUTH
TRANSEPT

HARCOAL
URIALS
(1896)

CHAPTER
HOUSE

BURIALS (1896)
BURIALS (1878)

SCHEDULED ANCIENT
MONUMENT BOUNDARY

ABBEY FOREGATE

182A

182

178-179

183-192 ABBEY FOREGATE

BURIALS
(1866)

'Abbot's Lodgings'

bey House

CHANNEL

1985
'B'

CHANNEL

MILL STREAM

BROOK ROAD

Abbey Pool & fishponds

A plan of the Abbey precinct: medieval and modern features.

Above: The iron waterwheel found intact inside the excavated nineteenth-century Abbey Mill. The sloping floor in the foreground is the base of a wheel bay from the earlier, seventeenth or eighteenth-century mill.

Left: The thirteenth-century precinct wall footings under excavation.

Chapter Three

Reconstructing the
medieval monastery

The contrast between the standing remains of Shrewsbury Abbey and some of the
better-known rural monastic sites - such as Fountains Abbey, or the nearby Haughmond
Abbey - could scarcely be greater. The same could also be said of other urban abbeys,
like St Werbergh's in Chester, or St Peter's in Gloucester, which became those cities'
cathedrals and thus retained their churches intact together with many of their buildings
and their old monastic precincts. At Shrewsbury, as we have seen, the nave of the church
was saved in 1540 for the use of the parish, but many of the monastic buildings were
rapidly demolished and everything else was left to the mercies of the urban and market.
And unlike a monastic ruin in remote countryside, derelict buildings at Shrewsbury Abbey
would always have been within easy reach of innumerable town centre building sites
needing sandstone for foundations and cellars: it may in fact have been a far cheaper
source of such material than quarries outside the town.

The consequence of these factors is that comparatively little of Shrewsbury Abbey has
been left standing. Nevertheless, several sources are available to us to reconstruct at
least a proportion of what has been lost. From the eighteenth century on, the remains
of the abbey had become of sufficient historical interest to attract the attention
of visitors, scholars, and artists, many of whom left written or drawn records of the
site and its buildings before the most destructive changes of the 1830s and 1860s.
The most important sources with which to begin the task of reconstructing the abbey
are the town histories of Shrewsbury published by Archdeacon Hugh Owen in 1808,
and by Owen and the Reverend J B Blakeway in 1825. This volume also contains
a measured plan made of the surviving remains of the precinct by John Carline junior,
a local stonemason and builder. The volume was also illustrated with engravings based
on sketches by John Chessell Buckler, one of the best antiquarian draftsmen of the
period. Buckler visited the abbey in 1813-14 and again in 1822, and his many
sketches (only a small proportion of which were engraved for the Owen and Blakeway

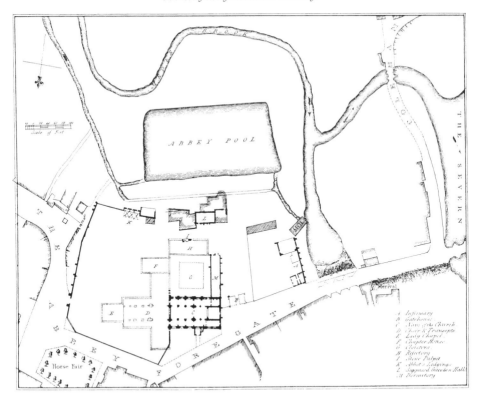

The 1825 plan of the precinct by John Carline Jnr
from Owen & Blakeway's History of Shrewsbury.
North, unusually, is at the bottom of the plan.

volume) are an invaluable source of information for buildings that were pulled down not long after.

Carline's 1825 plan shows the church as it is now, save of course for the additions made by Pearson in the 1880s; an outline reconstruction of the old east end is added, based in part on Owen and Blakeway's calculations of the length of the building from the plumber's accounts for the stripping of its lead roofs at the Dissolution. To the south of the church lay the cloisters, about 100 feet (c.30 metres) square, which would originally have been surrounded by buildings: the west range, the refectory to the south, and the east range, including the chapter house. By the early nineteenth century only the west range and the refectory pulpit were left. Although nearly all of the west range was demolished in 1836 for Telford's road, it appears in a number of engravings and sketches, notably Buckler's. These show that it was a long buttressed sandstone building with window and door-openings in a variety of architectural styles, and a timber-framed upper storey added at the north end after the Dissolution when that part

*Sketch by John Buckler of the abbey church
and the west range of the cloisters, 1813-14.*

was converted into a cottage. Owen and Blakeway thought that the west range had
once been the monks' dormitory, though this now seems an unlikely interpretation.
A tall narrow Norman window shown by Buckler suggests that at least that part of
Othe west range had been of one storey, possibly a hall that had once been part of the
accommodation for the abbot or his guests; the remainder of the range would perhaps
have been used for the storage of provisions under the supervision of the monastery's
cellarer. The real dormitory may have been part of the east range, perhaps with an
attached latrine block extending south to the watercourses, and may well have been
demolished entirely in 1540.

By 1825 no more was left of the refectory than survives today. Buckler's sketches
of the pulpit are most valuable for what they show of the buildings that stood
immediately behind it, to the south. This was the large, rambling private house known
as The Abbey or the Abbey Mansion. It incorporated the remains of a monastic guest
hall, shown on the 1825 plan, and a fine, richly-decorated, jettied timber-framed wing
built by the Langley family soon after the Dissolution; a fine drawing room was added
by Henry Powys in the 1760s to a design by Thomas Farnolls Pritchard. The building

Sketch by John Buckler of the refectory pulpit and the mansion behind it. Like many wealthy sixteenth-century Shrewsbury buildings, it was richly decorated, with carved bargeboards.

lasted until 1866, when it was quite unnecessarily demolished during the construction of Richard Samuel France's railway station. An outraged correspondent complained to the local press some years after that: 'the railway magnates spoke the word and the work of devastation commenced...reverenced by the historian as one of the remaining landmarks of our history, they were to the speculator a map of old buildings in shaky condition, and his ambition soared to replace them by a railway station, porters in tin buttons, and a weighing machine'.

The east range of the cloisters had disappeared entirely by Owen and Blakeway's day. The plan in their 1825 volume shows a rectangular outline representing the former chapter house, again based on the measurements of the leaded roof. They were not to know that the chapter house had actually had an apsidal, semi-circular, east end. This only came to light in 1896 when its curved foundations were spotted during excavations for a sewer down the middle of Telford's Abbey Foregate: the trench was dug from west to east, cutting successively through the footings of the west range, the cloister garth or garden and finally the chapter house; under the chapter house foundations lay charcoal burials, almost certainly part of the cemetery around the earlier wooden church of St Peter *(see Chapter One)*.

Just to the east of the Abbey Mansion the 1825 plan shows a group of fragmentary buildings, then a derelict stable, thought by Owen and Blakeway to be the remains of the Abbot's Lodgings. Sketched by Buckler in 1821, the ruins appear to have been part of the stone-vaulted basement storey or undercroft of a fine medieval building, lit by a series of three narrow windows in the south wall. The historians may well have been right in attributing these remains to the Abbot's Lodgings: they obviously represent a building of some wealth and importance, formerly with its principal rooms at first-floor level over the vaulted basement. Such an arrangement would not just have been well suited to the flood-prone precinct, it would also be entirely in accord with local fashions in high-status building in the thirteenth and fourteenth centuries. It was also situated towards the more secluded eastern end of the precinct, the most probable location for an abbot's private chambers in the later life of the abbey.

East of the cloisters, the 1825 plan shows only empty open space within the buttressed precinct wall. To an extent, this may reflect the medieval reality, for there is little doubt that this was the monks' cemetery. Skeletons have been discovered during building work on numerous occasions since the 1860s - under the main road, under the station

Early nineteenth-century view of the former cloisters. The west range (left) was partly rebuilt as a timber-framed cottage.

*Engraving of the abbey from the east,
based on a Buckler sketch. The old course
of Abbey Foregate curved around the
fourteenth-century precinct walls;
the blind corner was a menace for speeding
stagecoaches and led to Telford's 1836
short cut across the precinct.*

- now the car-park - entrance, and in the back gardens of the terraced houses next door. But the area has never been properly investigated, and it is highly probable that there were more, perhaps many more, buildings here. The real monastic infirmary, for example. The monks' infirmary would usually have been located towards towards the quieter, private, eastern end of a religious precinct, and one early map of Shrewsbury (John Speed's of 1610) bears the legend 'The Spittle', as in hospital, just east of the precinct. We know from the documentary evidence that the abbey infirmary was derelict even before the Dissolution, so it is not surprising to find that the building has disappeared without a trace.

The 1825 plan also shows the remains of the monastic precinct wall as it then survived east and south-east of the abbey church. South and west of the church we know from excavation and pictorial sources that the wall had been incorporated in or replaced by monastery buildings well before the end of the Middle Ages, but in the less built-up area east of the church the wall survived much longer, and it was sketched by John Buckler and others. The drawings show a high stone wall with a crenellated parapet: it may have been built with serious defensive intent, but is more likely to have been mainly symbolic, advertising the abbey's status as a great feudal landlord. Owen and Blakeway's account mentions that the standing wall was built on what appeared to them to be the softer, decayed footings of an earlier wall. This interpretation has been confirmed by an excavation which showed that the fourteenth-century red sandstone wall which still stood in the early 1800s replaced an earlier wall, built of a soft green-grey sandstone, built in the earlier thirteenth century *(see Chapter Four)*. The wall on the east side of the precinct was broken through by Telford's workmen in 1836 but a substantial section, including the postern gate illustrated by Buckler opposite the east end of the church, was left intact. It was demolished, for no very good reason, in 1841 and none of the wall now survives above ground.

West of the church and cloisters was a separate courtyard area extending as far as the 'Old Infirmary' buildings. The 1825 plan shows Owen and Blakeway's estimate of the site of the monastery gatehouse just west of the church; nothing more is known of it save for the appearance of what seems to be its Norman archway in the background of the Buck Brothers' engraving of the Old Infirmary *(see p.35)*. This also shows the remains of a range of buildings that extended east from the Old Infirmary along the north side of this courtyard to the church. What most of these buildings had been used for is not known, and they now lie under the main road between the Shrewsbury Quest and the church. They would however almost certainly have included the almonry, for the reception of the poor, as on better-known sites the almonry is almost universally found just within the main gate.

The courtyard itself was probably known simply as 'the court' or curia. A survey and rental taken of the former abbey precinct and Shrewsbury properties in 1540-1 noted 'the Courte', probably this area, 'environed with [surrounded by] lodgings and houses of office containing half an acre, worth little by the year by cause the clensyng [?stripping] of every office...'; a marginal note added that it was worth annually 3s 4d. There is nothing to indicate what functions these 'offices' once had, but again, better-preserved and better documented monastic sites provide some clues. Most monasteries were planned as a sequence of inward-looking courtyards, designed to give varying degrees of privacy and seclusion from the secular world outside. Many had an outer court, to house a range of functions that could include the storing and processing of agricultural produce, stabling, and almshousing. Many also had an inner court containing one or more guest houses, and where the inner court lay next to the cloister and its refectory, it would contain necessary service buildings such as a bakery and brewhouse, larder, and granary, under the watchful eye of the cellarer. The Shrewsbury Abbey precinct was very small by comparison with those of many Benedictine houses. As a consequence, its single courtyard west of the cloisters probably had to accommodate all the functions mentioned above, with the exception of agricultural processing and storage, which probably took place off site on the abbey's home farm or grange. Above all, the single courtyard seems to have been dominated by guest housing and the needs of victualling *(see Chapters One and Four)*.

To the south of the precinct lay the floodplain of the Rea Brook. When the 1825 plan was drawn, the floodplain was dominated by a single large pond called the Abbey Pool, separated from the former precinct by a subterranean water channel, shown as a dashed line. The pool was fed from the south-east by a leat or channel known as the mill stream, and from its north-west corner another channel led to the Abbey Mill next to the Old Infirmary. Excavations in this area, together with the earliest available maps, show that these arrangements represented a modified version of the water system that would have been familiar to the monks. In the Middle Ages there had been two fish-ponds lying side-by-side, embanked to keep out floods and fenced to discourage poachers. The ponds would have provided fish principally for the abbey's more important guests and for the abbot to present as gifts. Around 1800 the old fish ponds were amalgamated to form a single mill pond to drive the Abbey Mill, which was rebuilt at that time. Before, the Abbey Mill, and its unlocated medieval predecessor, had been driven directly by the mill stream, an artificial channel diverted off the Rea Brook about two kilometres upstream that also drove two further mills in the Abbey Foregate area *(see p.2)*. The mill stream formerly ran between the precinct and the fish-ponds. The subterranean channel on the 1825 plan - which passed beneath the Abbey Mansion's drawing room - was discovered by excavation in the 1980s, and appears to have been a drain using water diverted from the mill stream to flush the garderobes (latrines) of the domestic buildings, and perhaps the monastic dormitory, that clustered along the southern boundary of the precinct. The channel still existed, with water running through it, as late as the 1850s; its eastern end was probably destroyed during the construction of the railway station in 1866, though it could still be there, deep below the surface of the present car parks.

The ponds and channels in the Rea Brook floodplain demonstrate a typically monastic concern with good drainage and hydraulic engineering, a concern that also extended to the supply of fresh drinking water. Hugh Owen's 1808 town history mentions an 'arched aqueduct' which provided the monastery with water from a spring near St Giles' church at the far end of Abbey Foregate. This aqueduct was in fact an underground conduit, with stone walls and an unusual arched tile roof, that ran under the street. Just east of the precinct, in the street outside Cold Bath Court, there was a conduit head, presumably for the use of local residents, and this can be seen on the 1825 plan as a small square building. The water supply was still running through this system to the Abbey Mansion up to the time of its demolition, and a pump on the site of the conduit head was in use even later. The conduit was found in roadworks in 1895, and is said to have been seen more recently, but it has yet to be recorded by modern archaeology.

*The Shrewsbury
Saucer.
This shallow silver
bowl (diameter
133mm/5.25ins.)
is the earliest known
piece of English
hallmarked silver.*

*The Shrewsbury Saucer.
Close up of the leopard's
head stamp, the king's
mark for silver.*

Chapter Four

Excavating the medieval monastery

Early discoveries

The first recorded excavations within the old precinct took place in the early years of the nineteenth century, but we know little about them, or the people involved. An 1816 guide book to Shrewsbury mentions for example that 'in forming a garden on the site of the abbey cloisters a great variety of fragments were met with including the beautiful decorated tile floor of the refectory', found in front of the pulpit. Nearby, the footings of the west cloister walk and its Norman arcading were found, and further remains of the cloisters including a 'plain stone coffin' outside the south door of the church turned up a couple of years later. Whether these were all casual discoveries by gardeners, or whether someone was deliberately looking for antiquities and tracing foundations is not known. Most discoveries in the nineteenth century were certainly accidental, made during the course of building work, like the thirty skeletons found while building the railway station in July 1866, or the foundations and probable Anglo-Saxon burials found while laying a new sewer down Abbey Foregate in 1896. None of the major figures of late Victorian ecclesiastical archaeology excavated here as they did, for example, at the much better-preserved sites at Haughmond and Much Wenlock.

Major excavations in the 1980s
1. The Queen Anne House site

While there were one or two casual discoveries in the 1970s, nothing further of any great significance was discovered until the mid-1980s. Then, two redevelopment schemes were proposed. The first was for a new road (now Old Potts Way) to be built alongside the 'Old Infirmary' down the west side of the former precinct. The second - which in the end never took place - was for a commercial development on the old precinct itself, with new buildings sited in the blank areas on the 1825 plan on the assumption that these would be free of monastic remains. This assumption turned out to be wildly misplaced. To test the theory, a trial excavation was ordered in the back garden of the then derelict Queen Anne House, all now part of the Shrewsbury Quest site. A trench confirmed the presence of buried sandstone walls and deep, stratified, layers of soil containing pottery fragments and a wealth of other debris dating to the Middle Ages, and so, at the end of 1985, virtually the whole of the back garden was stripped of its topsoil by a mechanical excavator, and a team of up to thirty archaeologists began to dig by hand, peeling back soil layer after soil layer, removing the last traces of the eighteenth-century garden to reveal the tops of walls belonging to monastic buildings unseen since their demolition in the sixteenth century. This process continued for two years, by the end of which the earliest man-made layers had been removed and the natural subsoil had been reached, in places up to twelve feet (3.6 metres) below the modern ground surface. After the analysis of the stratigraphy (the sequence of soil layers), buried buildings, pottery and other objects, food rubbish and plant remains, it became possible to reconstruct in some detail the history of this small area of the abbey precinct and some of the activities that had taken place there, and in the surrounding area. From the earliest layers upwards, the story is as follows...

Apart from some stray sherds of late Anglo-Saxon pottery, the earliest detectable activities on this site probably took place in the late twelfth century. The natural gravel subsoil formed a slope down to the south, from the edge of the high, dry, natural terrace or promontory on which the abbey was founded, down into the Rea Brook floodplain, the lower, regularly-flooded area of watercourses and meadows. Cut into the gravel slope were four large holes dug to take vertical wooden posts, possibly part of some kind of fence or even a defensive stockade defining an early boundary to the monastery precinct. Outside this barrier and covering the bottom of the slope were thick layers of grey mud interleaved with organic material and sand. These deposits probably formed in a watercourse that flooded each year, submerging its surroundings and covering them with mud and with debris washed downstream. From seeds and pollen trapped and preserved in these waterlogged deposits, botanists were able to determine that the area was shaded by trees, mainly poplars, and that it dried out each summer becoming overgrown by nettles. From time to time someone, probably successive abbey janitors (such a post is recorded), tipped cart- or barrow-loads of rubbish there - a practice that was to continue on and off for another three hundred years.

If there was at first a wooden fence around the monastery, it was soon replaced by a stone wall, built of a distinctive if poor quality local sandstone. This took place some time in the earlier thirteenth century, and may just possibly have been a belated response to the attack on Shrewsbury in 1215 by Llywelyn the Great. His Welsh army is said to have avoided the heavily-defended Welsh Bridge on the west side of town and instead 'appeared suddenly before the gates of the Stone Bridge (English Bridge), where he set fire to the houses of the abbot' before capturing the town. The event led directly to the construction of Shrewsbury's town walls, and the abbey may have followed suit by building its own stone wall around the precinct. This wall too had

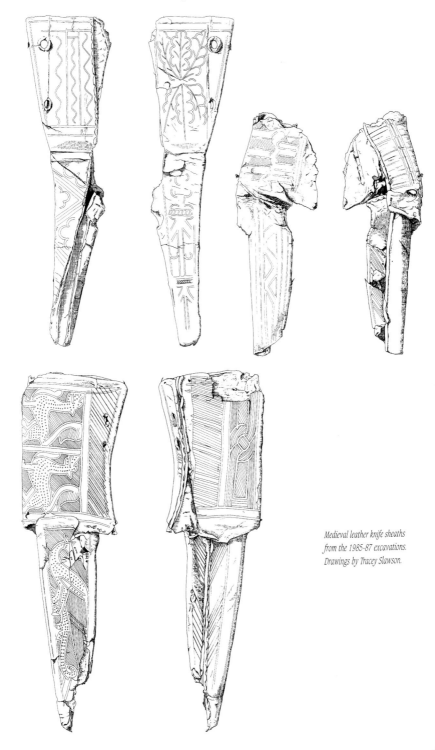

*Medieval leather knife sheaths
from the 1985-87 excavations.
Drawings by Tracey Slawson.*

but a short life. The base of what seems to have been a timber prop supporting it was found preserved in the permanently waterlogged low-lying area outside, and dated by its tree-rings to the years between 1268 and 1310. Soon after, a replacement wall was built of better stone. It was this second, fourteenth-century, wall that is known from the drawings of Buckler and others; part of it, together with a postern gate, survived on the east side of the abbey cemetery until 1841.

Within the precinct wall on the excavated site were the slight traces of former timber-framed buildings and the successive cobbled surfaces of the courtyards around them. The ground outside the precinct wall remained largely untouched, save by annual natural flooding and the continuing dumping of rubbish - and it is this that offers clues to some of the activities that were taking place in this part of the precinct. For instance, large cattle bones from most parts of the beef carcase were thrown there and suggest that cattle were butchered and probably actually slaughtered close by, presumably having been driven into the precinct on the hoof. Somewhere in the area imported luxury foods were being eaten, witnessed by fragments of almonds and a pine nut from the Mediterranean amongst more commonplace fruitstones and nuts. There were stables close by, evident from the preserved seeds and pollen of weeds that were imported with hay and straw, and deposited as dung and stable sweepings. Discarded scraps of leather harness, horseshoes, and two spurs confirm that horses and donkeys or ponies were accommodated here, and smithing waste suggests that there was a blacksmith or farrier nearby to service them. Other crafts were practiced in the area: cobbling, the repair rather than the manufacture of shoes, seems to have been a permanent feature of this part of the precinct, and for a while (in the twelfth-thirteenth centuries) there was a horn workshop, and a bone workshop.

It is the cobbling waste that brings us closest to the people who came here. One shoe upper still bears a cross-shaped cut made by its owner to ease the discomfort of a large bunnion. Probably the most important single observation has been that the size range of the discarded shoes show that women as well as men were having shoes repaired: the excavated rubbish on this site does not derive solely from the monastic community - their guests, too, are represented. A minority of the shoes found would have been considered fashionable, and the dating suggests that visitors to Shrewsbury Abbey followed London trends closely. Most, however, were practical working wear, and it is impossible to know whether these too had belonged to visitors - some perhaps footsore pilgrims - or to the abbey servants who worked here.

Interlude: the mystery of the silver saucer

In the mud outside the fourteenth-century wall, the excavators also discovered a small, shallow, grey metal bowl. Facetious comparisons to an ashtray ceased when it became apparent that it bore a hallmark, and was probably made of silver, a diagnosis subsequently confirmed by scientific analysis. The object was a silver saucer, a piece of very high quality medieval tableware that would have been used to hold sauces, and sometimes mustard, custard, or milk. They appear frequently in medieval inventories and other records, as, for example, in 1326-7, when Edward II had 279 plain silver saucers at Caerphilly Castle. The Shrewsbury saucer is stamped with a leopard's head, a mark which was specified in a statute of 1300 as proof that a silver vessel was up to the sterling standard; it is uncertain whether it was employed by provincial goldsmiths or only those working in London. The importance of the saucer is that, from its archaeological context, it is virtually certain that it was deposited before c.1400, possibly well before, making it the earliest piece of English hallmarked silver yet known. Unlikely to be a common monastic possession, it may well have belonged to a visitor of high status, quite possibly a royal visitor, of which there were several in the course of the fourteenth century. How it came to be in the mud outside the precinct - whether dropped by accident, thrown there in a fit of pique, or discarded to cover up a theft, is anyone's guess.

Rebuilding, c.1400

Sometime around 1400 a section of the precinct wall within the excavated area was partially demolished to allow for the construction of a new building projecting further southwards. The wet muddy ground outside the precinct wall was prepared for the new structure by having alder piles driven into it, and then new stone walls built on top. These formed the footings of a building about 12 metres square externally, with its ground floor surface raised well above most potential floodwaters. A stone slab-floored drain ran along the south wall, discharging westwards into what now remained of the low-lying wet area outside the precinct. There was probably a large fireplace centrally placed in its west wall, the outside of which was given a fine ashlar face.

Because of its high floor level, when excavated, all trace of the building's original fixtures and fittings were long gone. However, amongst the rubbish that built up in the remaining low wet area outside it were a number of fragments of pottery dripping pans - vessels usually associated with kitchens and with food preparation more than consumption. The form of the building (square, with a fireplace on one side) is also consistent with what is known of monastic and great house kitchens, which were usually centrally planned: often square, sometimes round or octagonal. From the site's position, well away from the monastic cloister and the refectory, but on the edge of the abbey court or *curia*, it seems that this new kitchen was not built for the monks, but for their guests. This is completely consistent with the picture that is beginning to emerge of building campaigns in the later 1300s and early 1400s concentrating on the western end of the precinct and - by implication - visitors to the monastery.

Outside the kitchen and the surviving section of the precinct wall, the low lying area appears to have remained a kind of forgotten corner, convenient for the occasional disposal of rubbish. A latrine, or garderobe, was built, projecting over the precinct wall

A late medieval latrine under excavation.
The wall nearest the camera has been removed.
Inside were silts rich in food remains,
the eggs of human parasites and rubbish,
including footwear.

with a stone-lined pit on the outside to receive the waste. Out of this material were
sieved the remains of cereals, together with fruit stones and pips, and human parasite
eggs. The botanist analysing these remains described them as classic late medieval
latrine deposits - 'a medieval fruit salad'. Close by a small shed was built, leaning
against the outside of the precinct wall, but we cannot tell what its purpose was.
It was certainly in an unsavoury location, built on ground that was now usually dry
but still used as an occasional dump for rubbish and latrine waste.

The food remains - principally animal bones - show that slaughtering was taking
place nearby more frequently than before. A wider range of animals was also being
consumed, and they included deer, rabbit and hare, fowl, goose, duck, grey heron,
mute swan, partridge, woodcock, and raven. The game species in particular suggest
that high-status guests were being fed, recalling the literary and documentary accounts
of feasting and lavish hospitality at the fifteenth and sixteenth-century abbey.
The kitchen itself probably remained in use for as long as there were visitors. And then,
at the beginning of 1540, it all came to an abrupt end. The new lay owner of the site,
William Langley, is recorded as having employed a number of journeymen tanners,

and the excavations were able to show where, and why. Cut into the floor of the kitchen building were two rows of stone and clay-lined tanks, only their bases remaining. The old kitchen had, it seems, become a tannery, making use of the supply of running water in the drain channel alongside the south wall. Whether the roof remained on the building during this phase is unknown, but the remains of the kitchen finally disappeared during the eighteenth century as the area was turned into a garden for the Queen Anne House; the channel alone survived well into the nineteenth century as an open ditch bounding the south side of the garden.

2. The Abbey Mill site

Few if any excavations take place just 'to see what's there' but some set out with a particular objective only to discover something entirely different and unexpected: the Abbey Mill site was just such an excavation. From the account in Domesday Book and from later records it is clear that milling was an important source of revenue for the medieval abbey throughout its life; it was granted three watermills at the time of its foundation and these, by implication, were already running before the abbey was built and appear to have been part of the site's late Saxon background *(see Chapter One)*. The last Abbey Mill, which burnt down in 1906, stood outside the precinct just beyond

*Eighteenth-century drawing of the
Abbey Mill, outside the 'Old Infirmary'.
Excavation confirmed the details
of the water channels seen here.*

the Old Infirmary, and its site was well known from a variety of sources, including the 1825 plan. When in the early 1980s proposals were advanced for the construction of a new main road with deep foundations across its site, excavations were planned which, it was hoped, would reveal a millennium-long sequence of watermills.

The ground south and west of the Old Infirmary was known to be wet, deep, and technically difficult to excavate, but at an early stage the outline of the last watermill was revealed. It was a rectangular brick building lying at an oblique angle to the abbey buildings, with two internal wheel bays, each supplied with water via large Victorian brick culverts. The wheel bay at the end of the building was empty, only the circular grooves worn in the side walls showing where the wheel had turned, but in the central bay the iron waterwheel was discovered intact, left in place when the building was destroyed by fire.

This mill had been constructed c.1800, and more or less the first record of it is its appearance on the 1825 plan, but it was known that it was not the first mill on that site. Eighteenth-century illustrations show a pair of somewhat ramshackle buildings either side of a watercourse, one timber-framed, the other possibly stone, with a shed-like structure enclosing the external waterwheels *(see p.63)*; it was thought that these buildings may, in turn, have been built on the remains of an even earlier mill. As the excavation progressed the wheel-bay floors and other fragments of these earlier buildings were discovered built into the last brick mill - but these were most definitely the first buildings on the site. For underneath was nothing but wet, grey mud, and not just any old mud, but mud that had been deposited slowly in a major watercourse as it silted up. This discovery prompted an immediate review of the historical evidence, from which it was soon apparent that the excavators had rediscovered the old channel of the River Severn that used once to flow between the abbey and Coleham Head, formerly Coleham Island, roughly on the line of the Victorian railway viaduct. In fact John Leland, antiquary to Henry VIII, provides an eye-witness description of it from his visit to Shrewsbury in 1539. By that time the channel had silted up to the extent that it was barely covered by water in summer. Leland described it as 'an arm of the Severn, that at dead low waters in summer scant fleeteth over the strand. There is a bridge of eight arches [the Monks' Bridge] over this arm, and after that it passeth through this bridge it straight meeteth again with the great stream [the present main river channel]'. It seems that what had begun as an open, navigable river channel became slowly choked with silt in the course of the Middle Ages: the obstruction represented by the piers of the Monks' Bridge was probably a major factor in this. By c.1700 it was dry enough to be reclaimed, and a mill was built there to replace the medieval mill - known from Speed's 1610 map to be somewhere nearby, but as yet undiscovered. The knowledge that Shrewsbury Abbey was sited not just close to the Severn but actually on it is of considerable importance: it underlines the original strategic importance of the site, suggests how building materials were brought to the precinct, and offers an explanation of the very unusual architecture of the 'Old Infirmary', particularly the arcaded west elevation that appears in so many illustrations.

3. Further discoveries

During the 1990s several excavations took place to record buried archaeology in advance of building work: all this work was on a much smaller scale than that in the 1980s, but nevertheless adds many useful new pieces to the still very incomplete jigsaw puzzle. In 1993 work on the Shrewsbury Quest site commenced with the digging of a number of trenches to find out how far down new foundations could be taken without disturbing buried medieval remains. These trenches, and others dug the following year, were the first opportunity to explore the surroundings of the standing Old Infirmary buildings. They showed that, beneath the topsoil, much of the area is covered by layers of sandstone and mortar rubble from the demolition of former abbey buildings; beneath that are the remains of the buildings themselves, and the rough, almost farmyard-like, cobbled yard areas in which they stood. What was surprising was how many buildings there once were. Although wall-footings and floors could only be glimpsed in the small trenches, it became clear that the Old Infirmary is just a fragmentary survivor of a dense, complex clutter of buildings occupying the south side of the former abbey court or curia. On the south side of the Old Infirmary, as it is now approached by Quest visitors, was at least one building with a stone-flagged floor lying along the inside of the old precinct wall; some buildings probably stood for centuries, others perhaps for only a few years; at least one was destroyed by fire. These very small-scale samples of the medieval abbey at the moment add just a little to its history, but warn future archaeologists that very complex remains await further exploration below the reconstructed herb gardens of the twentieth century.

Further reading and research resources

For a detailed account of the abbey precinct, the archaeological excavations, aspects of the abbey's history, and specialist reports on the excavated finds (the silver saucer and other artefacts, botany, animal bone, building materials and so on), the reader is referred to Shrewsbury Abbey, studies in the archaeology and history of an urban monastery, Shropshire Archaeological and Historical Society monograph, edited by N J Baker, which also contains a comprehensive bibliography.

The basic documentary history of the abbey is contained in the Victoria County History of Shropshire,volume II, (ed. Gaydon, A T), 1973; for the 18th- and 19th-century history of the site this should be supplemented by the late Mary Owen's article: 'Before Beringar', in the Shrewsbury Civic Society Newsletter, summer 1993, pp.5-6; the Shrewsbury Abbey Cartulary has been transcribed and published by Dr Una Rees in The Cartulary of Shrewsbury Abbey, Aberystwyth, 1975. Owen and Blakeway's History of Shrewsbury vol.II, 1825, is still indispensable. The best account of the architectural history of the abbey church remains that by D H S Cranage in: An architectural account of the churches of Shropshire 2, part 10, Wellington, 1912. The wider context of Shrewsbury Abbey is admirably covered by Dorothy Cromarty's Everyday Life in Medieval Shrewsbury and Bill Champion's Everyday life in Tudor Shrewsbury (Shropshire Books, 1991, 1994), and by George Baugh's and David Cox's Monastic Shropshire (Shropshire Books, 1988). For mills and milling, see R A Holt's The Mills of Medieval England (Blackwells, 1988).

For further information on archaeological excavations and all other discoveries, the reader should consult the Shrewsbury Urban Archaeological Database, held by the Property and Planning Department, Shropshire County Council, The Shirehall, Abbey Foregate, Shrewsbury. A copy of the database is also held by the National Monuments Record, RCHM(E), Swindon.

The artefacts from the abbey excavations are on public display in the Medieval Gallery at Rowley's House Museum, Barker Street, Shrewsbury. Further primary documentary material, photographs, and other illustrations, are held by the Shropshire Records & Research Centre, Castle Gates, Shrewsbury.

Glossary

Abbey	A monastic community governed by an abbot or abbess.
Almonry	The monastic building dedicated to the reception of the poor, for the giving of alms.
Aisle	Part of a church flanking and parallel to the nave or choir, separated from it by an arcade.
Apse	The semi-circular termination or extension to a building, often at the east end of an 11th or 12th-century church.
Arcade	A series of arches.
Bay	The structural division of a building, usually emphasised by the placing of columns, buttresses, or windows.
Benedictine	Of the monastic Order of St Benedict (c.480-543).
Capital	The decorative top of a column, from which an arch or vault might spring.
Cellarer	Monastic official responsible for provisioning the monastery.
Chancel	The eastern part of the church reserved for the use of clergy.
Chantry	An endowment for priests or monks to sing masses; the chapel used for that purpose.
Choir	That part of the church used by the choir.
Clerestory	The upper storey of an aisled church, its windows lighting the interior.
Floodplain	Flat area bordering a river or stream that is subject to regular flooding from it.
Lady chapel	A chapel accommodating an altar of and dedicated to the Virgin, forming part of a larger church, usually at its east end.
Nave	The central space of an aisled building, usually a church, in monastic terms generally divided by a screen between the monks and the lay public.

Pier   A masonry column supporting an arch.

Transept   The short arms of a cruciform building, projecting north and south
              from the crossing.

Triforium   The first floor level of an aisled church with long chambers or galleries
              over the aisles communicating with the nave via arcades above the
              nave arcades and below the clerestory.

Undercroft   A subterranean or ground-floor space dedicated to storage or
              commercial functions below the principal living spaces of a medieval
              domestic building.

Index

More books on Shropshire's history from Shropshire Books

EVERYDAY LIFE IN MEDIEVAL SHREWSBURY Dorothy Cromarty	£7.95
EVERYDAY LIFE IN TUDOR SHREWSBURY Bill Champion	£7.95
SHROPSHIRE FROM THE AIR: An English County at Work Michael Watson and Chris Musson	£12.99
SHROPSHIRE FROM THE AIR: Man and the Landscape Michael Watson and Chris Musson	£13.99
HISTORIC PARKS AND GARDENS OF SHROPSHIRE Paul Stamper	£12.99
THE FARMER FEEDS US ALL Paul Stamper	£4.95
HISTORIC BRIDGES OF SHROPSHIRE Anthony Blackwall	£4.25

For a complete list of Shropshire Books titles please write to:

Shropshire Books,
Column House,
7 London Road,
Shrewsbury,
Shropshire SY2 6NW.